Big Machines in Space

by Brienna Rossiter

FOCUS READERS®

SCOUT

www.focusreaders.com

Focus Readers is distributed by North Star Editions:
sales@northstareditions.com | 888-417-0195

Produced for Focus Readers by Red Line Editorial.

Photographs ©: Shutterstock Images, cover, 1, 7, 9, 11 (top), 11 (bottom), 13 (background), 15, 16 (bottom right); NASA, 4, 13 (spacecraft), 16 (top left), 16 (top right), 16 (bottom left)

Library of Congress Cataloging-in-Publication Data
Names: Rossiter, Brienna, author.
Title: Big machines in space / by Brienna Rossiter.
Description: Lake Elmo, MN : Focus Readers, [2021] | Series: Big machines |
   Includes index. | Audience: Grades K-1.
Identifiers: LCCN 2020033606 (print) | LCCN 2020033607 (ebook) | ISBN
   9781644936702 (hardcover) | ISBN 9781644937068 (paperback) | ISBN
   9781644937785 (ebook pdf) | ISBN 9781644937426 (hosted ebook)
Subjects: LCSH: Space vehicles--Juvenile literature.
Classification: LCC TL795 .R684 2021 (print) | LCC TL795 (ebook) | DDC
   629.4--dc23
LC record available at https://lccn.loc.gov/2020033606
LC ebook record available at https://lccn.loc.gov/2020033607

Printed in the United States of America
Mankato, MN
012021

About the Author

Brienna Rossiter is a writer and editor who lives in Minnesota. She loves being outside and looking at stars.

Table of Contents

rocket

Blasting Off

A **rocket** blasts off.

It goes high into the air.

Going to Space

Rockets send things to space.

They shoot out fire.

They go very fast.

Studying Space

A space station stays in space.

People live inside it.

They learn about space.

Spaceships go to the

space station.

They take people.

They take supplies.

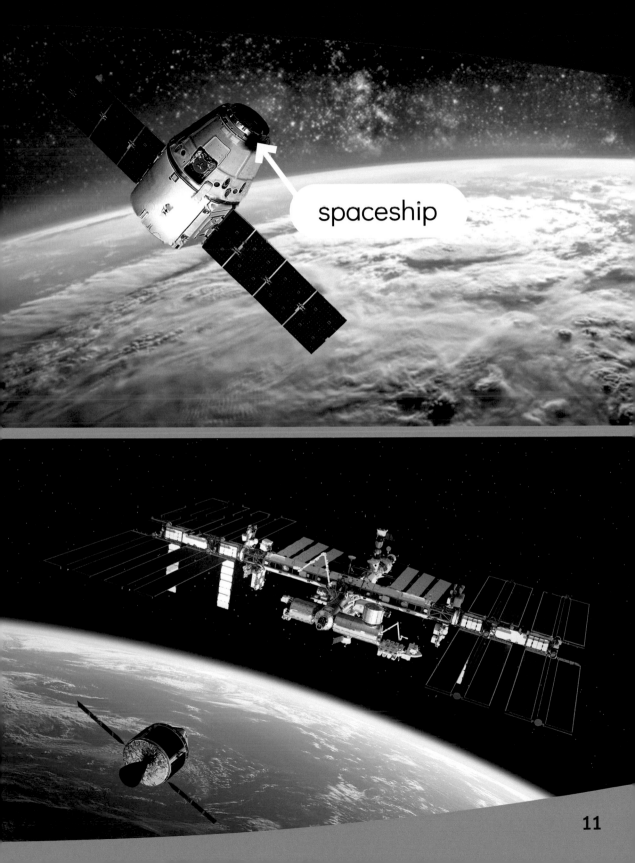

spaceship

Some spaceships go far
into space.

They study **planets**.

They study **moons**.

13

Some **telescopes** are in space.

They look for planets.

They look at stars.

They can see very far.

Glossary

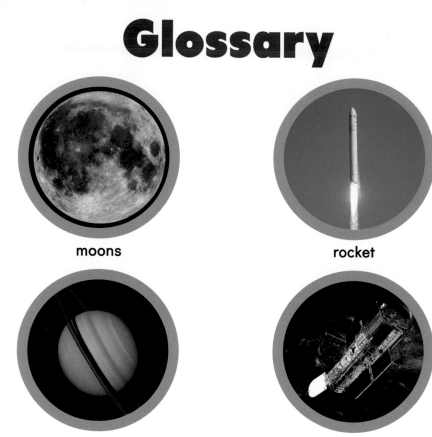

moons

rocket

planets

telescopes

Index